YOGI BERRA
Baseball Legend

"In baseball, you don't know nothing."

— Yogi Berra

He wasn't born Yogi. His name was Lawrence. Lawrence Peter Berra. When his mother started calling him Lawdie, so did everyone else.

Lawdie lived in St. Louis on The Hill, a neighborhood of Italian families. Times were hard and his neighborhood rough, so Lawdie grew up tough as leather. Good thing, too, 'cause of all the razzin' he got. Kids called him names because they thought he looked weird and talked funny.

Yogi lived for baseball. So what if they played games on an old dump. Who cared if they had to nail together broken bats and tape worn-out baseballs? Not Yogi. He was crazy about the game and dreamed of playing in the majors.

When he wasn't playing ball, Lawdie loved watching movies. In one film, he and his pals saw a yogi, a guy practicing yoga. The man sat with his legs crossed, just like Lawdie did. When his pals started calling him Yogi, so did everyone else.

Yogi loved baseball and movies. School? Now that was another matter. Yogi did lousy and saw no reason to get better. By eighth grade, he'd had his fill so he talked his parents into letting him quit. He'd make his living playing ball. Until then, he'd get a job.

And he did. He worked at a coal yard, on a Pepsi truck, and in a shoe factory. Problem was, he had afternoon ballgames. When Yogi cut out from work early, he lost one job after another.

Yogi lost jobs but his playing got better. That got him tryouts with the Browns and the Cardinals, but neither team knew what to make of Yogi. The kid could hit, but he swung at everything. He could throw, but he nearly fell over when he did. Yogi didn't even look like a ballplayer. So, he didn't sign on with either team. Some bigwig even told Yogi he'd never make the major leagues.

Yeah, what'd he know? A year later, a guy knocked on the Berras' front door. He worked for the New York Yankees. THE NEW YORK YANKEES! They wanted a catcher for their minor league team. Yogi—all of 17 years old—floated all the way to Virginia to play for the Norfolk Tars.

Far from his home, family, and friends, Yogi landed hard. The fans could have welcomed him, but instead they razzed him and called him names. All because of the way he looked.

This time, Yogi got sore. "This is going to happen," the manager told him. "More to you than others. If you ever show them that they're getting to you, you're dead. Ignore. That's what you gotta do. Ignore."

Joining the Navy wasn't enough for Yogi. No, he wanted to be in the action, just like on the ball field. That's why he volunteered to serve on the small boats that launched rockets during battles.

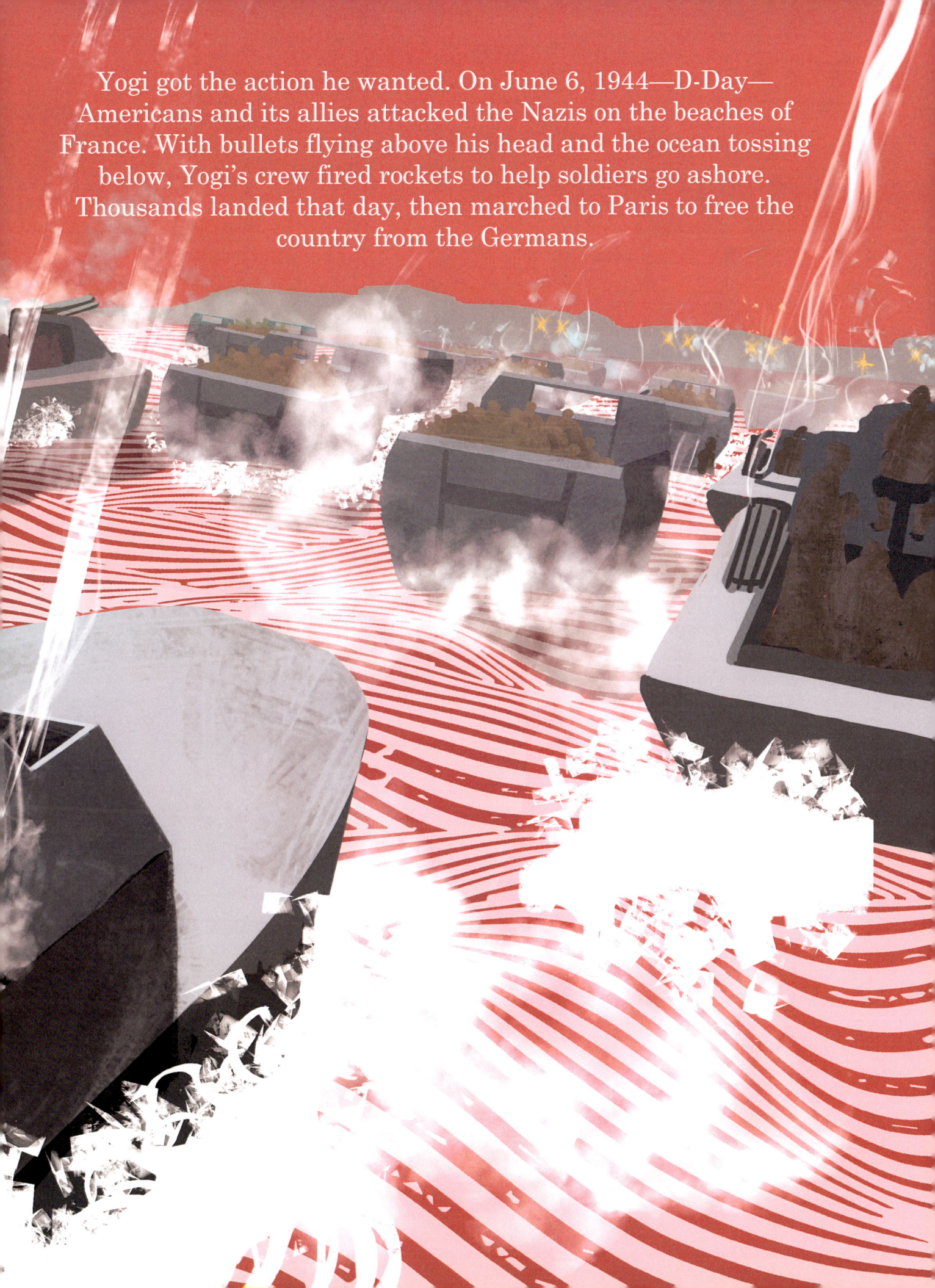

Yogi got the action he wanted. On June 6, 1944—D-Day—Americans and its allies attacked the Nazis on the beaches of France. With bullets flying above his head and the ocean tossing below, Yogi's crew fired rockets to help soldiers go ashore. Thousands landed that day, then marched to Paris to free the country from the Germans.

After the war, Yogi happily returned to baseball. But, when the Yankees sent Yogi to their minor league team in Newark, nobody thought he'd be any good. Why else would they give him a hat that didn't fit? Why would he get a uniform with no number on the back?

Yogi didn't get sore. He let his bat do his talking. Crack!—a single to left, Smack!—a double in the gap, Bam!—a home run! Soon, he got called up to THE NEW YORK YANKEES. In his first Yankees game, Yogi swung at a bad pitch and smashed it into the right field seats. Home run!

So, what did Yogi do? He laughed, joked, or pretended not to hear. Mostly, he kept hitting and helping the Yankees win games. Championships, too. They won the World Series in 1947, and were champs four of the next five years.

Behind the plate, Yogi became a force. His stubby body blocked wild pitches. His rifle arm gunned down runners trying to steal bases. And his mind, the one people thought wasn't too sharp, really was. Yogi used that razor-sharp mind to plan games, signal pitches, and even make history.

Fifth game of the 1956 World Series against the Dodgers. Don Larsen on the mound for New York, Yogi behind the plate. As batter after batter stepped up for the Dodgers, Yogi signaled the pitches and Don threw them.

"It's never happened in World Series history, and it hasn't happened since."

Not a single Dodger got a hit. Not one. Nobody even reached first base. Twenty-seven batters up, twenty-seven batters down. A **perfect game**, the only one ever thrown during a World Series!

Yogi won more than that. He won the Most Valuable Player award three times. He won a place on 18 All-Star teams. He played in 14 World Series and won ten, more than any other player in baseball history. Best of all, Yogi won over the fans. They came to love the way he talked, the funny things he said, and the way he played the game: hard and fair.

"When people ask me my greatest thrill, I say, which one?"
—Yogi Berra

So, what did people call Yogi then? They called him a great ballplayer, and the biggest winner in baseball history. And they still do.

Afterword

After Yogi's playing days ended, he stayed in baseball. He managed and coached the New York Yankeses, the New York Mets, and the Houston Astros, winning three more World Series rings along the way. The Yankees retired Yogi's uniform number—8—in 1972, the same year he got elected to the Baseball Hall of Fame. Yogi's one-of-a-kind face and his funny words became as famous as his playing. He was on the radio, TV, and in all kinds of ads. His funny sayings, called Yogisms, got repeated by people around the world.

In 1998, the Yogi Berra Museum and Learning Center opened its doors on the campus of Montclair State University in Little Falls, New Jersey. The museum celebrates Yogi's career and helps teach kids the values he lived: hard work, determination, and sportsmanship.
In 2015, Yogi Berra died peacefully in his sleep. He was 90 years old. Yogi's life ended, but his legend lives on.

Yogi Timeline

May 12, 1925 – Lawrence Peter Berra is born to Pietro and Paulina Berra in St. Louis, Missouri

1938 – Receives the nickname "Yogi" from friends

1939 – Drops out of school after eighth grade

1941 – Tries out for the St. Louis Cardinals and the St. Louis Browns, but doesn't sign a contract

1942 – Signs a contract with the New York Yankees

1943 – Plays first pro game for the Norfolk Tars

1944 – Joins the Navy and fights in World War II

1946 – Plays for the Newark Bears
    Called up to the Yankees; hits a home run in his first game

1947 – Becomes a permanent part of the Yankees
    Hits the first pinch-hit home run in a World Series game
    Wins first of ten World Series

1949 – Marries Carmen Short in St. Louis
    Son, Larry, is born

1951 – Son, Tim, is born
    Earns first MVP award

1954 – Earns second MVP

1955 – Earns third MVP

1956 – Catches first perfect game in World Series history
    Son, Dale, is born

1963 – Plays last game as a Yankee
    Named Yankees manager for the 1964 season

1964 – Leads Yankees to the World Series; fired after they lose
    Hired as a coach/player by the New York Mets

1965 – Retires from playing; keeps coaching

1969 – Mets win the World Series!

1972 – Elected to the Baseball Hall of Fame.
    Becomes manager of the Mets
    Yankees retire Yogi's number—8

1975 – Hired as a coach by the Yankees

1983 – Becomes Yankees manager

1985 – Fired by Yankees
    Hired as a coach for the Houston Astros

1989 – Retires from baseball

1998 – Opens the Yogi Berra Museum and Learning Center in Montclair, NJ

September 22, 2015 – Yogi Berra dies in West Caldwell, New Jersey

Bibliography

Barra, Allen. *Yogi Berra: Eternal Yankee.* New York: WW. Norton and Company, 2009.

Berra, Yogi. *I Didn't Say Everything I Said.* New York: Workman Publishing Company, 1999.

Berra, Yogi. Ten Rings. New York: HarperCollins, 2003.

Berra, Yogi. *What Time Is It? You Mean Now?* New York: Simon & Schuster, 2003.

Berra, Yogi. *When You Come to a Fork in the Road, Take It*! New York: Hyperion, 2002.

Berra, Yogi. *The Yogi Book.* New York: Workman Publishing Company, 2009.

Berra, Yogi. *You Can Observe A Lot By Watching.* Hoboken, NJ: Wiley, 2009.

DeVito, Carlo. *The Life and Times of an American Original.* Chicago: Triumph Books, 2008.

Dickson, Paul. *Baseball's Greatest Quotations.* New York: Harper Perennial, 1991.

Pessah, Jon. *Yogi: A Life Behind The Mask.* New York: Little, Brown and Company, 2020.

Shapiro, Ed, ed. *The Yale Book of Quotations.* New Haven, CT: Yale University Press, 2006.

Websites

https://baseballhall.org/hall-of-famers/berra-yogi

https://www.baseball-reference.com/players/b/berrayo01.shtml

http://www.biography.com/people/yogi-berra-9210325

https://yogiberramuseum.org/

A Look Behind the Scenes
These are some early exploratory sketches and illustrations working to define Yogi's style and visual aesthetic across the book

Early stage cover design

For
Tommy R. and Parker

With many thanks to Tom Reichert and Parker Snare for leading the way to Yogi; to Dave Kaplan and Eve Schaenen, Executive Directors of the Yogi Berra Museum and Learning Center, for their helpful feedback; to fellow authors Sheri Bestor, Kurt Cyrus, David Kelly, and Jonah Winter for their collegiality; to Mark Anthony Vega for his insights; to Lindsay Berra for the thumbs-up; and to Ava Litton for her eagle eyes and continued loving support.

The author deeply appreciates the creative vision, attention to detail, professionalism, and integrity of Marcelo Simonetti, who illustrated, designed, and laid out this book.

Published by Real Writing Press
978-0-9742196-6-0

Copyright © 2025 by Robert Young - www.realwriting.us

Illustrations by Marcelo Simonetti - email: me@marcelosimonetti.com

All rights reserved. No portion of this book may be reproduced or utilized in any form, or by any electronic, mechanical, or other means without the written permission from the publisher.

For permission, contact Real Writing Press at areswhy@gmail.com.